Contents

Any words appearing in the text in bold, **like this**, are explained in the glossary.

Writing a story

What is a story? A story tells the reader about a series of events. For example, a story might be about the things that happen to a person and to the people they know. This book will help you to get writing, so that your friends and family can read the exciting and interesting stories that you want to write.

All you have to add is your imagination!

Characters and plot

There are two ingredients that you will find in every story. Firstly, there are **characters**, who are the people in a story. They might be based on real-life people, or made-up people. We meet the characters as the writer tells the story.

The second ingredient is the **plot**. This is what happens to the people in the story. As a plot unfolds, we learn more about the characters and how they get on with each other. The plot should have an ending that leaves the reader happy, excited, surprised or sad – or all of these things!

Making stories interesting

Before writing your story, you need to think about what makes stories interesting. Here are three very important things that you need to know before you start:

- Your readers need to **identify with** at least one main character. Try to make them imagine what it is like being that person. Make them share the feelings of the character.

- You have to describe how characters in your story look and behave by using words alone. If you use words cleverly you can grab readers' imaginations and make them 'see' the characters. This is known as **descriptive** writing.
- You should **set** your story in interesting places. People can watch films or plays but when writing a story, you must create **scenes** by using words alone.

Activity – what makes a good story?

Think about stories you have either read or had read to you. Make a list of five things that you think must go into a good story.

Put your list in order of importance. Start with what you think is the most important thing to have in a good story. You can give examples from actual stories that you have read, if you want.

A *good story has:*
- *lots of action*
- *animals*
- *a mystery*
- *lots of interesting characters*
- *good descriptions of places*

Roland thinks the sound of screaming is important in a crime thriller.

Types of story

Stories can be about anything. That is why millions of books have been written. Certain types of story, called **genres**, have become popular. A genre is a type of story written in a certain style about the same sort of subject.

Here are some genres or types of story you might write:

genre	subject
Fairy tales	often have a hidden message, such as not to trust appearances
Fantasy stories	like complicated fairy tales, usually set a long way in the past or in a made-up world
Science fiction	often set in the future, with space ships, distant planets and future worlds
'Whodunnits'	mysteries where the reader has to work out who committed an act or crime
Ghost stories	scary stories about ghosts that frighten the reader
Horror stories	like ghost stories but usually with more blood and guts!
Stories about growing up	usually about love and about family life
Adventure stories	exciting experiences, usually with plenty of action

Top tip

Are you having difficulty choosing what to write? Then write about something you know, such as pets or pop music. The famous author Malorie Blackman's book 'Hacker' is a thriller about computers, which she used in her work before becoming a writer.

Collecting ideas

When thinking about what story to write, try keeping a writing journal. This is a book where you can note any rough ideas for **plots**, **scenes** and **characters**. Look around you, listen to people, and write down the things you see and hear. Here are some things that might help you with ideas:

- photos in books or magazines
- interesting or unusual names for people and places
- your feelings and what causes them
- ideas from other stories that you can mix together
- places that you visit
- an unusual person you have seen or met.

Activity – new stories from old

Think of a story that you have enjoyed. What genre was it? Find other stories by the same author by using the school library, local bookshop or the Internet. Are they the same sort of story? Is the author writing in one particular genre?

Now find the part of the story that you found most exciting. Try to write it in a different genre. For example, if you enjoyed the chapter describing someone being bullied at school, you could rewrite it so the characters are medieval knights. You could even write it like a story from a different land, or even set it in a different time. Soon you will have a completely new story!

Sir Swotalot drew his shining sword and challenged 'Slasher' Jones, the form 3Y bully, to a fight.

A story with a message

Most good stories have a subject and a theme. The subject is what the **plot** of the story is actually about. The theme is more difficult to explain; it is the idea or ideas behind the story.

What is the subject?

The subject of a story will have several parts. For example, the subjects of a good mystery story might include:

- an exciting mystery
- clues to keep the reader guessing about the mystery
- a main character who is trying to solve the mystery.

The theme

The theme is not part of the plot or action. It is the message of the story, something that the reader might think about after they have finished reading. For example, a story about a

dog rescuing its owner from danger has as its theme the love animals show to their owners.

A theme might make us think about how we should behave – for example, that people who do bad things often suffer for them in the end.

Top tip

Once you have chosen your subject and theme, give your story a title. Make it catchy. What title would you give a story about a best friend being caught for stealing? For example, 'Deep Trouble' would be much catchier than 'What Happened When Kim Brookes Got Caught Stealing'. You can always change the title later on.

Writing about what interests you

If you feel strongly about something, writing a story is a good way of telling other people what you think. For instance, if you think killing animals for meat is wrong, you could write a story about someone saving a lamb that escapes from a farmer's lorry. Your theme would be about how showing kindness towards animals is better than turning them into burgers!

Activity – developing your ideas

Here are some ideas for a mystery story.

> A family is staying on a farm for their holidays. There is an abandoned railway nearby. On certain nights, the family hear a train going along it. Is it a ghost train? Is something being moved around when it shouldn't be? A local person offers to help the family on the farm, but the family distrusts them.

The subject of your story is the mystery. The theme is about trusting people.

- What things could happen in the story?
- Who is the local person? What have they got to do with the old railway and the mystery?
- Why should the family be suspicious of the local person?

Now use your imagination to write ideas for a plot and some **characters**. What is the theme going to tell the reader?

Planning a story

You should always plan your story before you begin writing. You will find it easier to write the actual words if you know how your **plot** and **characters** will develop.

Basic ingredients

These are the main things you need to include in your story plan:

- Who are the characters in your story?
- Where is the story taking place?
- When is the story happening?
- What happens in the story? What is the story about?
- What events get the story going?

Putting it together

You should put all the main elements of your story in your plan. It is important to have a strong beginning and ending (see pages 14–15). The longest parts of a story are usually the middle **scenes**. They build up to the most exciting events or **climax**. The middle scenes also explain the events that **resolve** the story.

Many writers like to think of their plan in a shape, like this:

Exciting or key moment (a climax)
Cat goes missing

Events building up
What is wrong with it? Trying to find out

Events to sort things out
Hunting for cat

Opening or beginning
You get a pet cat

Ending
Cat returns with kittens

Story plans can have all sorts of shapes. You can build up events and resolve parts of the plots several times before the ending. You can also include exciting scenes called cliffhangers (see page 12), or add in problems that need to be resolved.

story shape with several climaxes

Top tip

Be careful you don't lose the **focus** on the main character. Readers like to concentrate on one person. You should always be thinking, 'Who is the main character in this story?'.

Polishing your plan

Once you have the basic events in place, you can think about moving scenes from one place in the story to another. Sometimes events make more sense in a different order! You don't have to stick exactly to your plan when you are writing. You can add new scenes, characters and events if you want. You can even change the ending.

Activity – making a plan

Look at the collection of ideas below. Pick out some to make a story. Identify ones that build up the story and ones that resolve parts of the plot. How would you arrange them in a story plan?

Write short descriptions of what would happen in each of the scenes. Then think about how you would link them to make a complete story plan.

> Gran tells her grandchildren a secret.

> Yesterday, a visitor arrived from abroad. She says she is a relative ...

> The new girl in our class seems rather odd.

> I found the mysterious box in the attic!

> Did we see a ghost?

> A letter with a photograph arrives in the post. It is not signed.

> Mum was hiding a parcel in the spare room.

> The box contained photographs and a letter.

Exciting scenes

To keep your readers interested, you need important events or **scenes** happening at regular intervals. Some scenes will be full of action, while others will develop events in a more gradual way.

Action paragraphs

Some of your key scenes might contain lots of action. Here are some ways to write good action scenes:

- Explain simply what is happening, using plenty of short sentences in your descriptions.
- Use strong **verbs** and **adjectives** to get the reader excited.
- Include exclamations, such as 'Help!', in your **dialogue** (see page 24).
- **Set** the action in exciting places.

> 'Smack!' The stone hit the windscreen like a bullet. 'Crack!' The glass broke into tiny pieces, a spider's web in front of the driver. Swerving wildly, the car went off the road and launched over the yawning cliff. It struck the rocks and bounced. Then it slammed to a stop. There was no movement. Nothing.

Cliffhangers

Writers often have a 'what will happen next' ending to a chapter. These cliffhangers make the reader want to move quickly on to the next part of the story. One way of writing cliffhangers is to have something dramatic happen to your main character then ask: *Was Colonel Stephenson still alive?*

Top tip

As a writer, identify your key scenes when you are planning your story. You can't go into great detail for every scene — unless you want to write a very long book! You should know which are the important scenes to concentrate on.

Key events

Exciting scenes don't have to be packed full of action to be effective. Other key events can make exciting scenes.

- One **character** could tell a story to another, or reveal part of a mystery.
- A character might suddenly show their true feelings for another character.

Activity – words, action!

Below is a fictional newspaper report of some strange happenings, long, long ago.

Use a bit of the information given to write a **paragraph** full of action. For example, you could write about the strange experiments in the castle, the giant figure leaving the castle or about how Mrs Bott saw the man with a bolt through his neck. Add a cliffhanger to the end of the action.

Black Rock Gazette
1 April 1812

STRANGE HAPPENINGS AT CASTLE DOOM

Last night, one of the citizens of Black Rock reported seeing strange lights coming from Castle Doom. As a storm hit the town, Morton Throck saw a bolt of lightning hit the castle tower. He saw a giant figure leave the castle, pull a tree out of the ground, and then walk into the valley. Other townsfolk believe that the castle is being used for odd experiments by Professor Strangelight. They have heard the sound of clanking machines. Mrs Bott, the madwoman who cleans at the castle, says she has seen a man with a bolt through his neck.

Beginnings and endings

All stories need strong beginnings and endings.
They must be well written and interesting to read.
Here are a few basic tips.

The beginning

The beginning, or opening, sets the tone (e.g. funny, scary) for
the story that will unfold. You could do any of the following:

- Describe the **scene** where the story begins. Let your readers
  'see' a picture of the place where it happens. It helps them
  get into the story. For example,
  *The dawn came quietly to the fair city of Tirion. First birds sang
  from the trees and crowded rooftops, then sunlight touched the
  palace towers.*

- Introduce the main character first. This lets readers know
  who is the most important person in the story. For example,
  *It was a nice day, but Rachel hated it. She was usually a cheerful
  girl – but now she wanted it to rain and rain.*

- Write strong descriptions, for example,
  *Suddenly, the stomp and snort of horses filled the crowded yard.
  Smoke slithered and weaved like fingers in the black frosty air.*

When you have written your opening scene, read it and think 'If
I was a reader, would I want to read on?' Writing strong
beginnings with lots of **descriptive** text can be hard work, but
it is very interesting to read. However, try not to write the first
scene in a certain way but then change your style when you get
into the **plot**.

Top tip

Consider setting your opening scene in a place you know. It is much easier to write
about a **location** you are familiar with, rather than one you have never been to.
You can change some of the details and names if you want to.

The ending

At the end of your story you should show how the plot is **resolved**. You should round everything up so it is a natural place for the story to end. The reader should feel that they have understood the whole story.

- If your story has a theme, is its message made clear?
- Don't end an exciting story with a disappointing twist like 'Then I woke up; it had all been a dream.' Readers will feel cheated!
- You could explain how your characters feel, or how their lives have changed.

Activity – grabbing the reader's attention

Choose one of the following types of story:

- a story about animals
- science fiction
- a story set among friends at school
- a ghost story.

Write a really good opening scene for the type of story you have chosen. It must keep the interest of your readers. Start with something like the line under the picture below.

No-one from the village ever went near Codford Manor after dark. Not since that dark winter's night a hundred years ago when old Jethro Slurry disappeared ...

Twists

People enjoy stories that have a twist or surprise. This is where something unexpected happens in the **plot**. It can be fun to shock your readers with a good twist.

Planning

Twists need very careful planning. Work out exactly where the twist will come in your list of **scenes**. It does not have to be the ending or even near the end – although many stories do have surprise endings. You can have a twist or surprise at any point in your story except right at the beginning. Readers need to be involved in the story and think they already know what is happening for a twist to work.

A list of twists

How about these examples of twists?

- A character in disguise shows their true identity – for example, a stranger turns out to be a long-lost uncle.
- The reader is made to believe one thing but is then given another explanation – such as, **characters** think that X stole the jewels, but the detective shows it was in fact Y who took them.
- The real reason why something happened is explained. For example, Dad explains that he was so angry when Ben ran away and got lost in the city streets because he did the same thing when he was Ben's age and was robbed.

Top tip

A good way to build up the **tension** before an exciting twist is to ask rhetorical questions. These are questions that writers don't really want an answer to. They are asking them to get people's attention. You can ask them to the reader – for example, 'Slowly, Lindy pushed open the door. Who do you think was behind it?'

Sudden or slow

There are two ways of bringing in twists and surprises:

- A sudden shock – *Suddenly, there was a hand on my shoulder. The mysterious stranger had crept up on me. It was my uncle!*
- Slowly build up the tension – *The detective gathered everyone together. 'Well, who did take my jewels?', said the princess. 'Patience,' said the detective, 'all will be revealed. I have to explain how I worked out the identity of the thief …'* The detective explains in detail before naming someone nobody expected to be the villain.

@ Activity – What's the twist?

Note down the main scenes for a story with a twist. The story will be **set** in school, and someone has played an amazing trick. What is it? No-one knows who has done it. Who is responsible? Why have they done it?

Come up with a twist, so that we really believe the wrong person is going to be blamed. At the last minute we discover that the trick was played by someone we did not expect.

Just who was it that had managed to put a giant eel in the school pool? And why did they do it? One thing was certain, no-one in Class 4 wanted to try and get it out!

Believable characters

The **plot** is very important in a story. But just as important are the **characters**. They should seem like real people with their own likes and dislikes, habits, moods and ways of talking.

What are they like?

When you are planning your story, decide what your characters are like.

- What are their names? For example, Wild Phil Hiccup would be a good name for a sharp-shooting cowboy – but not so suitable for a ballet dancer.
- Are they young or old?
- What do they look like? Are they tall, bony, bald, blue-eyed? Don't just think about their height, clothes and so on. For example, imagine the way they move or sit.
- What sort of personalities do they have? Are they usually happy, nasty, confident?

You can help the reader to picture a character by making something about them unusual. But don't make them so odd that they are not believable!

Inner thoughts

Knowing how a character is feeling is important. Don't just say *Ray was frightened*. How frightened? Think of all the ways you can describe being frightened, from a bit unsettled to terrified and shaking. Ask yourself why Ray was frightened and imagine how you would feel.

Top tip

Think about how your characters speak, and create different **voices** for them. One character might speak in a very posh way, another might use more slang.

Behaviour

If you have planned your characters well, you should know how they would behave in a situation – just like you know what your friends and family would do. Decide how your characters will act towards one another. If something awful happens, will the characters help each other?

It helps if your characters behave in a way the reader expects them to. For example, a heroic doctor will probably be polite and try to do good things.

Activity – inventing characters

A young boy sees a vampire running into an old castle. Then a man in a white coat follows him, carrying a crocodile. He looks round nervously before he closes the castle door. A whistle blows, and a police officer charges up, bangs on the door and dives in. The boy wonders what's happening and goes inside.

Who is the vampire? Who is the man in the white coat? Why has the police officer followed them and what does he intend to do?

Write a story using the events and **characters** above. Make your characters sound as different as possible when they speak.

Now add one new character. How will he or she be different from the others? Will your character change the way things happen as the **scene** develops? Write notes on each character before you start if that helps.

Descriptive writing

Readers like action, but they also want to know what places and **characters** look like. To do this, writers use **descriptive** writing to 'paint' exciting pictures in their readers' minds.

Making pictures with words

It is easy, but dull, to write descriptions that are just 'Okay' because you've not really used your imagination. Don't use the first words that come into your head to describe something.

For example, if you want to describe a tiger, don't just say that it was big and strong.

- Say exactly what you are describing, for example *Bengal tiger*, not *big cat*. Exact descriptions are called precise nouns.
- Find exciting **adjectives** like *fierce*, *sleek* and *powerful*.
- You could describe how the Bengal tiger moves, using powerful **verbs**, such as *prowling* or *stalking*.
- Or you could put together words that sound alike – *with silent steps, the stripy hunter stalked the shadows*. This is called **alliteration**.

Top tip

When you describe something, do not just write about what you can see. If you are describing a town, mention the sound of traffic as well as people talking and shouting. You could also bring in the smell of the shops and describe the feel of the cold wind on your face.

Similes and metaphors

One way of writing short but exciting descriptions is to use **similes** and **metaphors**.

A simile is when you say something is 'like' something else, or where 'as' is used to make a comparison. For example, *the stairs were as slippy as ice*. A metaphor is when you describe something as if it was something else. The metaphor *a mountain of work* is a good description of the way homework seems to pile up!

You can also describe things as if they were people, for example, *the chattering fax machine*. This is called **personification** and can make objects come alive.

@ Activity – churning stomachs

Your school goes on a trip to a famous theme park. The most terrifying roller coaster there is the 'Stomach Churner'.

Imagine you really don't want to go on it, but cannot back down in front of your friends. Imagine walking towards it. Describe the sounds and sights. You get closer to the ride. It towers up into the sky. Describe what it looks like to you and how you feel, up to the moment when you get into the car and it moves forward.

Now, instead of being frightened, imagine you really love roller coasters. Describe what it looks like to you, and how you feel, as you get ready to ride the 'Stomach Churner'.

People are screaming with fear. They shriek like frightened birds.

People on the ride yell with excitement. The air is a storm of happy sounds.

Who's telling it?

There are two main ways of telling a story from different points of view. You can be one of the **characters** explaining what is happening. Or you can be a **narrator** floating about everywhere in the story but not actually part of it.

Writing as a character

You can tell a story as if you are one of the characters. You describe things as they happen to you, which creates excitement. You write things like *I opened the box* and *I was afraid*. This is called writing in the **first person**.

The disadvantage of writing as one of the characters is that you can only say what your character is seeing and feeling. You have to guess what is going on in other characters' heads. You can not be in **scenes** where your character does not appear.

Being a narrator

Being a narrator means you can sort of 'float' in the story.
- You can see into every character's head.
- You can say how each character is feeling.
- You can describe scenes happening at the same time in both Britain and in Australia!

See the difference?

Here is someone writing in the first person, as a character:
I saw Mr Wilson going towards his car. He was carrying something, but I could not see what it was. It was raining hard and the water was pouring down my neck.

This makes us feel part of what is going on, as it happens. We share the character's thoughts. The same scene written from the point of view of a narrator would be like this:

Spencer watched Mr Wilson carry something towards his car.

Spencer was getting soaked and couldn't see that Wilson was carrying a big metal box with the treasure in it.

This is more like a report. We don't feel so much part of the scene. But we can include information (what Wilson was carrying) that Spencer cannot see.

Activity – points of view

Imagine you find a dog hiding in an old shed. He is frightened, hungry, enormous and lovely. You decide to take him home. Your mum is scared of animals and your gran is allergic to pet hairs. You leave the dog in the garage. Then you and a friend try to persuade your mum to let you keep the dog.

Write what happens as if you are the person who finds the dog and takes it home. (Use phrases like *I heard a growl ...* and *Raoul and I opened my front door ... .*)

Now write the same scene as if you are a narrator watching all the characters. (Use phrases like *Sam and Raoul heard a growl ...* and *Raoul opened the front door ... .*)

Now, just for fun, try writing the scene as if you are the dog!

Happening right now

Sometimes you want to write down exactly what two or more **characters** are saying to each other. This is called writing **dialogue**.

Writing dialogue

Dialogue is written in **direct speech** and in the **present tense** so that things seem to be happening right now. It makes the story more exciting and immediate. For example, your story might go:

'Look out!' shouted Joe. 'The road is flooded. Stop over there and I'll look for a boat.'

This is much more interesting than writing **indirect speech** in the **past tense**, like this:

Joe said the road was flooded. He asked the driver to stop and said he would try to find a boat.

As you can see, 'speech marks' are put around the words that are actually spoken.

Top tip

When you write dialogue, try to 'hear' each character's **voice** in your head. Get their way of speaking into your writing. Remember, what characters say doesn't have to be in perfect English!

Using indirect speech

Dialogue can be a problem because it can take an awful lot of writing to cover a whole conversation. Indirect speech lets you cut out a lot of the boring details. A good general rule is to use indirect speech for the basics, such as people greeting each other or discussing less important things. Then, go into direct speech to write dialogue when characters say important things.

Activity – developing dialogue

Look at the following **plot** idea:

A school party is on a weekend trip to the mountains. One character is a street-wise city kid who thinks the country is just mud and sheep. He is loud and confident at school. Now he is about to go pony trekking. The city kid won't admit it, but he is really scared.

Someone else, a shy boy at school, loves the country. He has already made friends with his pony!

That night, after the ride, the two of them start talking. Both are out of their usual world. What do they say to each other?

First, write their conversation as dialogue, all in direct speech. Make up any details you need to develop their characters. Think about how they got on during the pony trek and bring this into the conversation. Make sure each character has a different voice, a different way of speaking.

Now imagine you are someone who hears their conversation. Write about it in indirect speech, reporting what you heard. You can still bring in details about the characters.

25

Breaking it up

Really big blocks of writing put the reader off. They are too long to understand in one reading. Learn to use **paragraphs** to break your writing up. Paragraphs are the building blocks of **scenes**. They will help your reader see the individual events that make up your **plot**.

Moving things on

When do you need a new paragraph?

- Start a new paragraph every time the action moves on, when the story moves to another **location**, when time moves on, and when a **character** appears or disappears.
- You should also start a new paragraph when you move from a description of action to a description of the thoughts in someone's head.
- Start a new paragraph each time you start or finish using **direct speech**.

Sometimes your story might move backwards in time. For example, your main character might recall what happened to them in the past, which is called a flashback. You might need one or more new paragraphs for a flashback or you may confuse your reader about what is in the past and what in the present.

How long should a paragraph be? There is no rule. Sometimes just a couple of lines will make a complete paragraph. In a very important and event-packed scene, you might feel the writing needs to run on longer.

Top tip

You need to link your paragraphs so that your story flows smoothly for the reader. Try to connect them up by saying things like 'Later that day …', 'Then the gorilla burst in …', and 'Meanwhile, on the other side of town …'.

Activity – an opening scene

Read these notes for the opening of a story.

Jules has gone to the seashore with his family. He is exploring the beach when he sees an old fort on the cliff top. It is not a big castle, just a tower. He finds a path up the cliff, through scrubby plants and rock. At the top, the path winds round the tower. He goes in. There is a stone staircase up to the roof. He climbs up. He looks at the view and sees a woman he does not recognize. She shouts something at him, but he cannot hear what she says. She is waving at him from the beach. It looks like a warning, not a friendly wave ...

Write out this long opening scene in lots of detail. Describe the beach, cliff tower and so on. Say what Jules feels at different points. Divide up the sequence of events into paragraphs. Aim to have about six paragraphs.

Polishing your story

When you have finished writing, read through your story. Try to imagine you are reading it for the first time, as if someone else has written it. Only then will you be able to make fair judgements about its good and bad points.

How does it sound?

Always read a finished story aloud, with a pencil in your hand. Mark up bits that sound really good, and also the bits that do not seem to work so well. The following checklists will help you ask yourself questions about your story.

Plot and theme

- Did you have a theme in mind for this story? Have the ideas behind the story come over clearly?
- What things in the **plot** worked well? Can you make them even better? If the aim has not really been met, what is missing?
- Have you tied up all the loose ends of the plot?
- Does the story come to an end that is satisfying and natural?

The way you have written it

- Do **paragraphs** break up the plot so that it is easy to follow?
- Is the story enjoyable and interesting to read?
- Is the opening **scene** strong so it makes you want to keep reading?
- Have you described things well? Did you succeed in 'painting' pictures with words?
- Is the title still right for the story?

Characters

- Are the **characters** believable? Do your descriptions help the reader see how they look and what sort of person they are?

- When they speak in **dialogue**, do they sound like they have different **voices**? Read the dialogue out loud to get an idea of this.
- Do you care about the main character and what happens to them? If you do not, why should your readers?

Presentation
- Is your spelling, punctuation and grammar correct?
- Will readers be able to understand your handwriting? Is the story laid out clearly? Make sure readers can follow your words – you could try word processing your text on a computer.

Activity – making revisions

Look at the story or stories that you have now written. Look at the bits you marked up as being good. Can you see why they seem to work well? Now look at the dull bits. What is wrong? Re-write these pieces to make them better.

When you have made your revisions, you can present your story to your friends and family.

The scene where the two friends go to the market should be funny and interesting. But it's dull. I've described all the market stalls … but I haven't said how they felt about everything they saw. That's it!

Glossary

adjective word that describes something or somebody. For example, *a hot drink.*

alliteration putting together words starting with the same letter or sound. For example, *a slithery snake slid.*

characters the people you create to be in your story

climax most exciting point or key moment of a story

descriptive using words to describe something in a creative way

dialogue words two or more characters speak to one another. The exact words they use are written down in direct speech.

direct speech using the exact words someone says. For example, *'I'm going to the shops', said Sarah.*

first person writing as yourself by using the word *I*. For example, *I opened the box.*

focus concentrate on something

genre a style or type of story. For example, mystery stories and science fiction stories.

identify with feel close to or involved with a character

indirect speech reporting what someone says. Indirect speech does not use the exact words of the person speaking and is also known as reported speech.

location place where the scene is set

metaphor description of something as if it were something else. For example, *a poppy bruise*, describes bruised skin as if it were a red poppy flower.

narrator 'character' who tells the story through their eyes. A narrator can see into every character's head and describe how they are feeling.

paragraph section of a piece of writing, usually indicated by starting on a new line with a gap before it

past tense using verbs to explain things that happened in the past. For example, *Helen <u>jumped</u>* is in the past tense.

personification giving human qualities to objects or things, such as *the Sun went to sleep behind a cloud*

plot flow of events and scenes that make up a story

present tense using verbs as if something is happening now. For example, *Sajid <u>is</u> writing* is in the present tense.

resolve decide or find an answer to a problem

scene section of a story set in one particular location

set where the story takes place

simile a comparison of two things to make an image. For example, *the Sun was like a furnace.*

tension excitement that makes someone feel nervous

verb word that describes an action that someone in a sentence does. For example, he *runs*, she *was walking.*

voice in a story, the way a person speaks or expresses themself

Find out more

The following books are examples of stories written in certain genres. Try reading them and then get writing for yourself!

Malorie Blackman, *Hacker* (Corgi, 1993). A thriller about computers.

Michael Morpurgo, *King of the Cloud Forests* (Egmont Books, 2001). An adventure story set in 1941.

Websites

<u>http://www.stonesoup.com</u> is the website of a magazine, Stone Soup, which contains stories by other children from all over the world.

<u>http://www.mystworld.com/youngwriter/</u> is the website of Young Writer Magazine, which also features stories by other children.

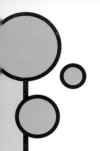

Index